MASTERY WITHIN 11:11

Integrated Master Numerology

Daphney Antoine

ISBN 978-0-692-13780-2

JPC Publishing

Book design by Antony David
Back cover photo by Humberto Vidal
Edited by Charlyne V. Schaub
Quote photos by Daphney Antoine

www.imnmastery.com

Welcome

"What you seek is seeking you" -Rumi

May these pages help you connect to your mastery within. Thank you for coming along on this inspiring, life empowering, numeric connection journey. I dedicate this book to all of you who are seeking self-knowledge to gain a greater understanding of life.

This book will educate you about Integrated Master Numerology and teach you how to work this numeric knowledge into your daily life. Following the numeric values that string and connects us has significantly changed the way I experience and take on my day. My goal is to make the information about Integrated Master Numerology easy to understand.

A lot of hours, collaborations and long focused work has gone into creating the processes in this book. This new knowledge aims to be user-friendly and is meant to help you with your numeric expansion. I am honored that I was open energetically to make this numeric connection. May you be open to your numeric expansion potentials.

Dedication

I dedicate this book to my mother, Romaine Esperance who allowed me to explore my own truths from a very young age. She never questioned my spiritual journeys. Each direction I took, she supported me, and never judged the many paths I've explored. To my kind, beautiful, loving children, my why, I strive to continuously improve myself so that I may be the mother you deserve. To all who supported me and kindly helped me along this journey, I send you blessings always for sharing your loving energy with me. I dedicate this book to the unified energy that unveiled the numeric processes and knowledge in this book. To you who are seeking self-knowledge and spiritual enlightenment, I thank you.

Your mastery lies within,
Let's begin the journey of discovery!

Introduction

What is Integrated Master Numerology (IMN)? IMN is a numeric process that helps you identify number's energetic pull. With the understanding of numeric attributes through Energy, Frequency, and Vibration, you can see the way you interact and experience numbers in your life. Our numeric codes influence our physical and non-physical experiences. While on my soul-searching and spiritual re-connection journey, I attuned to the IMN knowledge during my meditation.

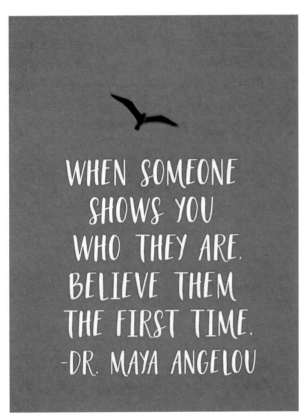

My spiritual journey began shortly after the birth of my daughter in 2012, the year I prayed for "Truth." I didn't know the significance of the truth until much later. There's a quote by Jack Nicholson from the movie *A Few Good Men* that said, "You can't handle the truth!" In my case, I had no choice, but to handle, and live with the unpleasant events that were unfolding. For me to understand the truth, I had to endure many difficult lessons and contrasts in my life. The revelations were utterly unexpected and unsolicited consciously. I was seeking the truth, expecting, and hoping it would keep my life intact; instead, my reality was to be on a different path from my expectations.

During that period, those I loved dearest showed up with their truth. Truths I didn't want to see or accept until I remembered a quote by Dr. Maya Angelou that

Oprah quoted in an interview "When someone shows you who they are, believe them the first time!" Believing them the first time was a painful lesson I had to learn.

Life Choices

In grueling, life-altering situations many seek external help; I went inward. I had this innate knowing to explore my own truths. I chose to walk the path - peace of mind, heart, and spirit! I dealt with my pain through meditation. During that period a dear friend Karina introduced me to guided meditation (a process where one or more participants meditate in response to the guidance by a practitioner or teacher, either in person or through sound recording). Karina owned a business in the same plaza near my business. We connected deeply through spirituality. We discussed her spiritual journey and my past interest in inner development. Karina was a real blessing, she never focused on my challenging predicaments. I believe she was placed in my life to help keep me balanced and connected with my Source Creator (God).

My Intro To Guided Meditation

The meditation Karina shared with me was the full audio of Abraham Hicks's *The Law of Attraction*. It had a life-altering effect on me. The first time I listened to the guided meditation was tough, and hard for me to focus. It almost hurt. I felt like my mind was going a million miles a minute; although, the voice in the meditation commended a calm state of mind. I eventually encountered fear during the meditation. I remember asking myself "What if this is a sin?" My fear mind was doing the driving. My organized religious belief came out fighting hard to maintain my limiting beliefs. I had to somehow find the strength to combat the guilt I was feeling in attempting to quiet my mind. I stayed committed, and somehow along the way, I felt ease, and I surrendered to the meditation. Once I was calm, I was able to experience a peaceful state of mind. By allowing the mind to be still, I experienced a beautiful feeling of unification. My regular committed meditation practices prepared me to go deeper within. I found alignment with my true self, and blessings began to show themselves.

The deeper I grew into my meditation practices, I knew I had to make drastic changes in my life. Especially, with conditions that triggered me to express uncontrollable thoughts. One day, while washing dishes, I found myself immersed in negative self-talk. I was blown away by all the different directions the mind can go while conducting a simple task. I had to find a way to stop this negative self-talk. If I wanted to grow personally and spiritually, I had to learn to love myself and not allow outside circumstances to trigger me negatively. I had to make radical changes and find ways to create a more inner focused, positive state of mind. Focusing on my positive aspects was not easy. I found strength through faith, guidance, love of self, and my children. I learned to embrace life challenges with these simple words "I love you enough to ignore you." I was determined not to feed negative energies. I took control of my situation and the negative chatters (The chatter has not gone... only now I am able to change the content to a more positive tone). Once the realization of staying positive was established, I was well on my way to incredible growth and processes. With my new focused, positive state of mind, it was as if a "START NOW!" Button got switched on. I intuitively knew a button was pushed, some would say the light switch went on. Life was about to take me on a new course where I could be in a new flow, and I was ready!

Nightly I listened to guided meditations or my favorite AUM (OM) chants (a sacred sound defined as "the sound of the universe" and a spiritual icon in Hindu religion. It is also a mantra in Hinduism, Buddhism, Jainism, and Sikhism). I listened, meditated or fell asleep with the AUM chants running through my earphones. My nightly practices opened me up spiritually, and through those nightly rituals, I developed a spiritual connection beyond anything I could have imagined. I made a sacred bond with a higher perspective.

Receiving Of The Numbers

To compliment my meditation practices, I started going to the beach every morning to observe the sunrise and meditate. It rained the morning of July 4th, 2015, and I couldn't go watch the sunrise. I stayed home in bed and meditated. During my meditation, I was shown the meaning of two groups of numbers 1-9 and 11-99. I had an awareness of numbers and an interest in their relevance. I'd browsed through a few numerology books, so I knew a bit about Numerology. Whenever I was trying to understand people and events, I would refer to numbers. I understood and respected the vision I received.

In the past, I found that the definitions of numeric meanings were always too complicated and wordy. The information I was receiving was simple and easy. Which is why it's my profound desire to keep the information I am sharing with you simple and easy to comprehend.

The Catalyst – Quantum Connection

An enlightened spiritual journey always encompasses a catalyst. My catalyst for this divine guided process came when I attended a three-day Science and Spirituality conference on Vancouver Island. On my last day, I met a woman while I was out for my last walk. It was a lovely day. By chance, we both stopped to observe a sunlight street artist (a practice called Solar Pyrography -someone who uses the

ray of the sun and a magnifying glass to burn on a piece of wood like a stencil form to create mind-blowing artworks). We were amazed and mesmerized at the young man's talent he was demonstrating. We started talking, it didn't take long for us to realize we were on the island for the same conference. We decided to go for tea to share our conference experiences and ideas. We discussed our reasons for attending the conference. She explained why the event was relevant to her. I expressed my need to connect with people in the spiritual community because of the connections I've made with the numbers. We spoke about the numbers and their definitions and the way I had received the vision during meditation. At one point, she stared at me in a state of contemplation and with ease, she said, "So it's Quantum Numerology?" I was baffled by the question. I asked "Quantum Numerology?" I was already exposed to the Quantum concept because of my exposure to Gregg Braden's lectures. I understood the implication of what she was suggesting and, it made sense. I believe our conversation was an opportunity for me to go connect more dots.

Mastery Within These Pages

Realizing and connecting to Integrated Master Numerology was a love project that took over three years and many hours of meditations. The 11:11 illumination awakening ran deep for me within the numbers. Ever since the number's relevance to the quantum connections came together I've used them as a tool to guide my life. Between these pages, I share the numbers and their definitions as I received them in my meditation.

This book offers 12 tested tools to help you create a better relationship with yourself, home, money, and love. You will be introduced to the concept and practice of Integrated Master Numerology - IMN. Once you have cognized the methods in this book, you'll be able to apply them to your daily life experiences. You will learn about the differences between Energy, Frequency, and Vibration. You will understand how important they are in improving your daily life. All the sections are easy to read and understand. I was deliberate in my intentions to follow the K.I.S.S structure (Keep It Simple & Sturdy!) With so much love, I am excited to share this knowledge.

Blessings always,

DAPHNEY ANTOINE

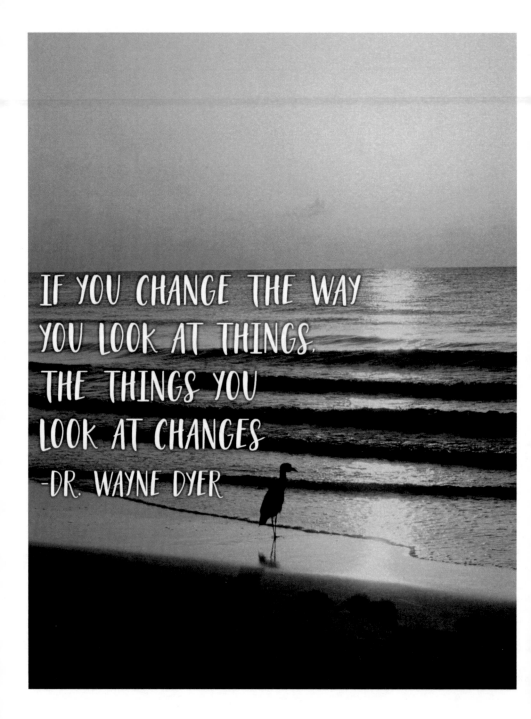

I AM

The Becoming

The becoming is the allowance of awareness of the self and internal growth. The self-actualization process is vital in any personal and spiritual development. I believe in the aspect of philosophy that deals with the principles of cause and effect. That belief caused me to be on this long quest to learn more about myself, esoteric teachings, and to understand what transcends the physical and non-physical realm of reality.

My decision to focus on my inner self led me down unexpected paths that required discipline, commitment, and dedication. Along the way, I had to deal with fear, lack of confidence, and self-doubt. I was patient, I knew and trusted there was a higher power at work. I learned to believe in something bigger than myself and accept what came. Acceptance was not easy, I had to make sure in my acceptance I didn't play the victim role. I had to learn how to appreciate and love without judgment.

For my birthday, I gifted myself tickets to a spiritual workshop which touched briefly on "Angel" numbers. I've always been fascinated by numerology, but numerology and angels were new to me. The meanings and significance of the messages in numbers discussed in the workshop captivated my attention. I just knew it mattered. It was a regular practice of mine to add everything from names, house numbers, and date of births. Now, I'm being told there are angel messages in numbers. *Yes*

After that workshop I started to notice numerical coincidences in my daily activities like waking up at 4 a.m., 4:44 a.m. or the time on the clock would add up to a 4. A bit bizarre, but I loved the coincide4nces. (The 4 which mean Spirit appeared in the word, so I kept it.) *There are no coincidences*

Change In My Understanding

On February 28, 2015, I came across a channeled audio message titled "Not Your Father's New Age." By Kryon through Lee Carroll on YouTube. Since I was on my spiritual quest, the title caught my eyes. I relaxed back to listen. WOW! From the moment I heard the voice, I felt a profound impact, and the message changed the way I looked at my reality. Days later, I wondered if Kryon would be coming to Florida, where I live. I typed Kryon into Google, "The Brain" as I fondly refer to it. To my amazement, I discovered Lee was channeling Kryon in Miami, Florida the same morning I discovered Kryon on YouTube. I couldn't believe the title of the workshop in Miami "Congratulations – Connecting the Dots." What an awesome coincidence! Considering I was trying to connect the dots. I continue to listen to Kryon, and through his channeled messages I was reintroduced to the concept of master numbers in Numerology.

I believe in divine guidance, and it fueled my desire to find out everything I could about the master numbers 11 - 22 - 33 - 44 and their energies about cause and effect. While I was listening to a video about master numbers it stated that master numbers only go up to 33 and at rare times 44. I had a strong sense there was more to the master numbers, a deeper meaning that had not yet shown itself. Immediately, I grabbed a piece of paper and wrote out 44 - 55 - 66 - 77 - 88 - 99. I felt gratified as if I knew something more significant. I placed the piece of paper on my bookshelf thinking I would find the clarification later.

Receiving The Numbers

I love to go to the beach for my morning sunrise meditation. It helps me connect with nature. On July 4th, 2015 it was raining too hard, and I couldn't go to the beach. I decided to meditate in bed. During that morning meditation, I connected to a higher knowing and perspective, which was showing me numbers. I realized the information was an elevated numeric knowledge. I jumped out of bed to write it down because I was concerned I would lose the connection and forget the information. I frantically looked for a pen. It was difficult to maintain the contact since it was my first time experiencing something like that… I was nervous, eager and excited!

The Numbers

As soon as I was ready to write, I heard the words "This is your first channel." I wrote as fast as I could and only worried about what I was writing later. When I was done, I was stunned! What I had written in my journal were two sets of numbers: 1 - 9, and 11 - 99.

Channeled 7-4-2015
The Numbers and their Meanings
Number definitions precisely the way they were received

Channeled
7-4-2015

1 - You are God "The I Am"

11 - God here and on the other side. Acknowledgment of your Source Creator.

2 - You and the other side of the veil. "your higher self."

22 - Connection of the two and the blend.

3 - Mother - Father - Child "Aspect of creation, the Trinity"

33 - The family is together, the most powerful to achieve.

4 - Spirit pure

44 - All spirits are together with loving support.

5 - New beginning & nature calling

55 - New beginning in life, spirit, and nature

6 - Energy

66 - Physical and non-Physical energy

7 - Knowledge

77 - Secret knowledge and codes [science number]

8 - Divine

88 - unlimited divine connection the type that creates New World - Power -

9 - Working with God - Creator

99 - Acknowledgement of God's work. Witness Beauty-Love & Light

7-4-2015

(journal entry after I wrote the numbers and their definitions)
This morning I woke up to go to the beach, it was raining too hard, so I decided to do a meditation. During the meditation, I saw Metatron with the Cube over his head which is how I knew it was Metatron. What an amazing experience. During the meditation, I was told, "Dark had to be in order for the light to appear." I totally got it. I was amazed by the message. Then I received another vision, I saw a white gate beyond the clouds and a flash that said, "The power is in the 1 (one)." I did not understand, so I moved my attention from it, then I got August 19 - as usual I did my calculations, and I said to myself it's 1 (one) the 9 (nine) removes itself.

After I hear "9 (nine) means you are working with God." When I would get numbers before in meditation, I would say to myself "I need to look the number up, I do not know the meaning." This time I was being given the meanings. I got out of bed and felt the need to write down what I was told. While looking for a pen, I was also told that this was my first channel and heard "spirit felt laugh at my collection of notebooks". For some crazy reason, I could not find a pen. I looked in my bag I found a blue pen, then I heard "blue pen as if by accident, where do you think you got that from?" I was looking for my black pen. I looked back at my journal the only time I used a blue pen happen to have some type of numerology reference.

Now What?

After I was given this higher perspective for numbers, I would get urges to pick up my phone, and I would see: 11:11 - 2:22 - 3:33 - 4:44 - 5:55. This would happen so often I could not ignore them. I started to capture screenshots of them on my phone. It became second nature. Whenever I would see the numbers, I would try to pay attention to what I was doing at that moment. I did whatever I could to make a connection between my actions and the numbers. I wanted to see if I could link a specific message to each occurrence.

I learned that numbers are the Universal language. I gained a new understanding through my exposure to the numbers. I took the time to understand that language through the definitions I received and their possible connected factors. Now it was up to me to figure out how to share the knowledge and meanings.I knew what I was given is meant to be shared.

Clock Screenshot

Friends I told about this phenomenon started to see the numbers randomly on their phones and clocks. They would call me to ask for the meanings; I enthusiastically shared even though I hadn't fully formulated what I had at hand. My friends knew that, and they still welcomed my interpretation of the meanings. During that time, I realized I was using my intuitions while explaining the possible messages. I faithfully documented the numbers while seeking a deeper understanding of the synchronistic relationship between the numbers and events

I Think I'm Done!

July 4th, 2016, I pronounced myself done! I spent one year observing the numbers. With a sense of responsibility, I felt the need to get the information out as soon as possible. I wrote affirmations corresponding directly to the numbers with the idea they would be included in a book about me receiving the numbers. . .

Tool #1: Affirmations

Affirmations help you affirm what you want and connect you to a higher perspective. The dualistic aspect of the master numbers enables you to tap into something more significant than the physical experience. The 11:11 reoccurrence calls you to take a moment and witness the beauty in your reflected self. The Quantum Affirmation Wheel is linked to the amplified aspect of the core meaning and vibration of each number. Find the number or topic you feel connected with or the theme you would like to affirm. Once you've identified your desired affirmation, recite the double-digit compliment to amplify the power. Recite daily until you feel you've achieved your purpose.

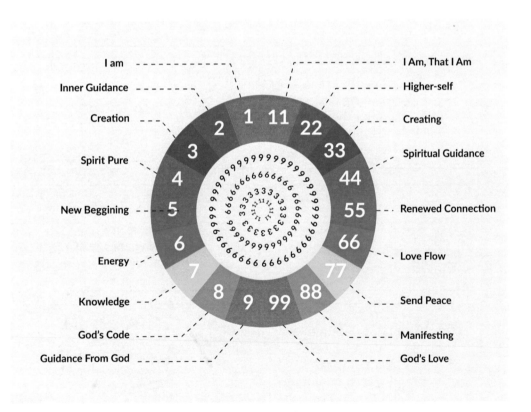

Affirmations

 I Am one with Oneness.

 I Am that I Am, I know my true self. I Am connected to my Source.

 I Am my greatest asset. I Am coupled with my power within.

 I Am joined with my greater knowing. I Am tapped into my inner guidance, I Am influential.

 I Am the creator of my reality. I honor the Mother - Father - Child aspect of creation.

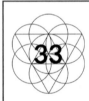 I Am celebrated by my creation. I Am supported by my spiritual family.

 I Am well guided and protected.

 I Am never alone. I reside in the loving energy of Spirit Pure.

 I Am welcome to change. I Am in harmony with my best potential.

 I Am Love! I love myself and humanity, I Am in harmony with my true nature.

I Am in the flow of energy. I am fueled by expanding energy.

 I Am in the energy of my Source field. I am flowing and vibrate with pure love.

 I Am an incredible processor of knowledge. I Am expanding daily.

 I Am wise. I am connected to a higher knowledge I chose Peace.

 I Am in the flow of my abundance. I give love freely, and I receive love effortlessly.

 I Am a master at manifesting. I Am in tune with my abundance, my desires flow freely to me.

 I Am working with God. I Am connected with Source Creator (God).

 I Am worthy of love. I Am blissfully experiencing Beauty, Love, and Light.

MASTERY TAKEAWAY

11:11 Thread Of Awareness

ENERGY: 11 is the Energy of illumination, a reflection of you and your potential.

KNOWLEDGE: The mastery within the 11:11 re-occurrence is a new level of conscious awareness. 11 11 aligns with the I Am presence. It shows you are ready to see the God inside.

WISDOM: Whenever 11:11 or any double-digit number sequencing presents itself, we tend to stop and take notice. We can't help acknowledge their presence. What I've noticed is the numbers only show themselves when we're feeli8ng (8 means Divine) good or in a good place. This feeling shows you are in alignment with your higher self. The greatest achievement is your alignment to God's codes of awareness.

DUALITY IS ALWAYS SECRETLY UNITY.
- ALAN WATTS

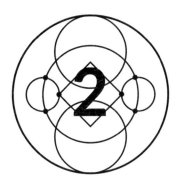

DUALITY

In The Numbers

Duality deals with opposites, like light and dark, up and down, old and new. In my case, the dualistic aspect showed up in the *Emerald Tablet* by Thoth. While I was planning this book, I stumbled on this old wisdom from Thoth which shows there were values placed in numbers. This gave me insight to the new wisdom I got in my meditation. I could not believe the many ways this ancient text validated what I'd received. I realized the journey had not even begun. It was apparent that more ingredients were being added to this soup, and more dots had to be connected.

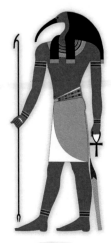

Thoth

Emerald Tablet
of Thoth

Thoth played many vital and prominent roles in Egyptian mythology, such as maintaining the Universe. From the Emerald Tablet: "Their antiquity is stupendous, dating back some 36,000 years B.C. The author is Thoth, an Atlantean Priest-King who founded a colony in ancient Egypt, {and} wrote the Emerald Tablets in his native Atlantean language which was translated by Dr. Michael Doreal."

The Emerald Tablets of Thoth-The-Atlantean
Tablet III

The Key of Wisdom

"Masters are they of the great Secret Wisdom,
brought from the future of infinity's end.
Seven are they, the Lords of Amenti,
Overlords they of the Children of Morning,
Suns of the Cycles, Masters of Wisdom.
Formed are not they as the children of men?
THREE, FOUR, FIVE AND SIX, SEVEN,
EIGHT, NINE are the titles of the Masters of men."

THREE holds the key of all hidden magic,

creator he of the halls of the Dead;
sending forth power, shrouding with darkness,
binding the souls of the children of men;
sending the darkness, binding the soul force;
director of negative to the children of men.

FOUR is he who loses the power.
Lord, he, of Life to the children of men.
Light is his body, flame is his countenance;
freer of souls to the children of men.

FIVE is the master, the Lord of all magic -
Key to The Word that resounds among men.

SIX is the Lord of Light, the hidden pathway,
path of the souls of the children of men.

SEVEN is he who is Lord of the vastness,
master of Space and the key of time.

EIGHT is he who orders the progress;
weighs and balances the journey of men.

NINE is the father, vast he of countenance,
forming and changing from out of the formless.

"Meditate on the symbols I give thee...
Turn thy thoughts inward.
Close not thy mind to the flower of Light.
Place in thy body a thought-formed picture.
Think of the numbers that lead thee to Life.
Clear is the pathway to he who has wisdom.
Open the door to the Kingdom of Light."

Once I finished reading the passages on the numbers from the tablet, I realized the dualistic worlds of the numbers. After my exposure to the Emerald Tablets, I stopped everything I was working on for the book. This new and exciting revelation reinforced the importance of the numbers, and I thought to myself. "This is intense stuff and why me?" I felt like the veil had been lifted and it was my turn to make it work and share this newly-found knowledge.

This was all so exciting. I needed time to process. Two thoughts continuously ran in the back of my mind, "What do I do with all this? How do I link it all together?" I couldn't believe it when the Tablet stated that "THREE, FOUR, FIVE AND SIX, SEVEN, EIGHT, NINE are the titles of the Masters of men." Really?

The Emerald Tablet dates back some 36,000 years B.C. In the preface, it states: "They should be read, not once, but a hundred times for only thus can the true meaning be revealed. A casual reading will give glimpses of beauty, but the more intensive study will open avenues of wisdom to the seeker."

Dare I read The Emerald Tablet 100 times to get the beauty?

Notes to self:

MASTERY TAKEAWAY

Influencing Reality

ENERGY: 22 is the Energy of your awareness of the physical and non-physical aspects of life.

KNOWLEDGE: The mastery within the 22 is the alignment to the higher self.

WISDOM: This vibration has the ability, foresight and knowledge to impact perceptions. The relationship with the greater knowing allows you to intuitively connect you to a dualistic perspective. This energy knows how to tap into the hidden inner-self and potentials. Be conscious and deliberate to your orientation. Trust your higher self and align with the empowered high-energy aspects of the collective.

CREATION

The Catalyst

Finding the message from Thoth was a needed, well-appreciated confirmation and the catalyst for me to want to learn and know more. Reading the Emerald Tablets a few times helped me develop a profound admiration for numbers. I became dedicated to learning whatever I could about numerical influences. My connection and respect for the numbers and their meanings became amplified.

While staying focused daily with the awareness of the numbers and their working in our lives, I was shown more potential for the numbers. I'd get messages in dreams, meditation, sometimes while driving or when I'm doing the dishes. Doing dishes is a great time to get connected - such a mind-numbing exercise.

Learning how to work with numbers and sharing the knowledge with others was a priority. The more I shared, the better I was able to explain accurately and with confidence, "what does it all mean?"

What does it all mean? *Numerology - Master Numerology - Integrated Master Numerology*

Numerology

nu·mer·ol·o·gy : n(y)o͞omə'räləjē

Noun - the branch of knowledge that deals with the occult significance of numbers.

mas·ter: mastər

Noun- a skilled practitioner of a particular art or activity.

in·te·grate: in(t)ə‚grāt

Verb - combine (one thing) with another so that they become a whole.

Numerology takes all numbers and reduces them to a single digit, e.g. (12) 1+2=3 or (27) 2+7=9. The single digit numbers range from 1-9. The digits 1-9 with each number having its own meanings.

Master Numerology leaves all double-digit numbers alone; like 11-22-33-44 it's suggested not to reduce to a single digit because those double digits show mastery in vibration. Master numbers are exceptional and require attention.

Integrated Master Numerology deals with numbers 1-9 and 11-99 and encourages you to align to the double-digit. The observation of numbers gives you the ability to align with the amplified characteristics of the double-digit. In Integrated Numerology, all numbers are unique with active Energy, Frequency, and Vibrational attributes. This alignment enhances the power in the numbers and intensifies their characteristics and tendencies.

Applying The Numbers To Your Daily Life.

Tool #2: Date of Birth Calculation

IMN calculates the birth date in two ways to ensure that if a master double digit is present, it will be seen in one of the two calculations. Here are two examples to show the two numeric calculation results.

NOTE – Nikola Tesla's birth date and Albert Einstein's birth date show different results.

Nikola Tesla Date of Birth: July 10, 1856
07 + 10 + 1856 = 1873 (1+8+7+3 = 19) (1+9= 10) (1+0=1)
1 Life Number

Or

0+7+1+0+1+8+5+6 = 28 (2+8=10) (1+0=1)
1 Life Number

Albert Einstein Date of Birth: March 14, 1879
03 + 14 + 1879 = 1896 (1+8+9+6=24) (2+4=6)
6 Life Number

Or

3 + 1 + 4 + 1 + 8 + 7 + 9 = 33
33 Life Number (This calculation shows the master number)

Take your time and calculate your own birth date. See examples to show you how to calculate

Calculation Space

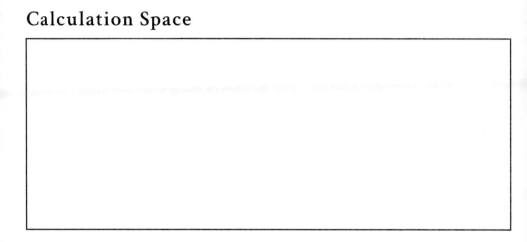

Tool #3: Age Sequencing Marker

My connection with the numbers surfaced broader than I could have imagined. I know one thing for sure: release all expectations, be open, and allow information to flow through.

The next obvious step was to start examining the possible correlation with our birth dates. The association of birth dates to the numbers was what I had to figure out. "Ask you shall receive!" Received I did, one more powerful component.

Let's start with something simple - the Age Vibration, calculate the current year minus the year of your birth to determine your age vibration.

2018 – 1974 = 44

Age Chart: The Age Chart helps you quickly identify your single digit and master digit age. Locate your age in the chart and look to the above YELLOW numbers, which show the single digit vibration of the numbers below. The GREEN numbers represent the master numbers and should not be reduced. The RED numbers add up to 11 mastery number.

IMN Age Chart

AGE CHART

1	2	3	4	5	6	7	8	9
10	11	12	13	14	15	16	17	18
19	20	21	22	23	24	25	26	27
28	29	30	31	32	33	34	35	36
37	38	39	40	41	42	43	44	45
46	47	48	49	50	51	52	53	54
55	56	57	58	59	60	61	62	63
64	65	66	67	68	69	70	71	72
73	74	75	76	77	78	79	80	81
82	83	84	85	86	87	88	89	90
91	92	93	94	95	96	97	98	99

How To Use Age Chart

Yellow boxes are the single digit reduction for the numbers below

Green boxes are all amplified numbers. (Do not reduce)

Red boxes add up to 11 (Do not reduce)

Life Cycle

December 2016, during an intense, emotionally charged conversation with someone I knew very well, I realized that there was a clear pattern in his life. Specific actions were drastic and potentially traumatic. I went to the numbers to understand what was happening. I identified a 9-year pattern because I knew him well. He demonstrated bold moves every 9 years. While I was trying to make sense of what I was observing, I realized, whatever I am seeing in him, is also present in me. At that point, I started to look at myself and my life patterns. Subsequently, I made an astonishing discovery. By examining my past patterns, I was led to the revelation of the numeric Life Cycles. The numeric Life Cycle is active in all our lives. This was a massive revelation.

Tool #4: Numeric Life Cycles

Life Cycles help you examine your past patterns. Think about a minimum of 3 or maximum of 9 major events in your life. (Events don't need to be in order). Write down your most memorable experience in the chart provided, and for each event list the year and reduce the year to a single-digit. For example, look at the first signifi8cant (8 means Divine) event. How would you describe it? What year did the event happen? How old were you? Do the same for the rest of your memorable life events. When you're done, take a moment to examine what you've written to help you identify patterns in your numeric Life Cycle see examples.

*** *All examples are from test subjects* ***

Example 1

Life Cycles

Year	Single Digit	Life Events	Age	Single Digit
	7	1/5/1945 My birthday		
	22	5/2/1923 My mother's birthday		
	22	10/9/1920 My dad's birthday		
1960	7	1960 I met My first husband	15	6
1969	7	1969 I met My third husband	24	6
1993	22	1993 I had my "Third Eye" opened	48	3
2009	11	Moved to my current home, house number energy 7	64	1
2014	7	Mother died, first trip to Arizona and Mt. Shasta	69	6
2018	11	First husband died, long time partner died, I met members of my soul group	73	1

In this example you can see that 22 and 7 are the dominant Life Cycle energetic influencer's. Also, you can see the synchronistic connections of the 1-age energy and the 11-year energy. This would say to me that there's a potential for mastery in the Dualistic aspect in Knowledge and an awareness of self-mastery potentials.

Example 2

Life Cycles

Year	Single Digit	Life Events	Age	Single Digit
1989	9	Eastern Bloc Revolution	23	5
1992	3	Moved to France	26	8
2002	4	Moved to USA	36	9
1996	7	Father passed away	30	3
2005	7	Mom died	39	3
2012	5	Birth of my daughter	46	1
1985	5	First marriage	19	2
2005	7	Second marriage	39	3
2007	9	Left corporate environment	41	5

In this example you can see that 7 and 3 are the dominant Life Cycle energetic influencer's. This would say to me that there's a potential for mastery in Knowledge and the ability to Create with awareness of I AM as the underlining 1 energy.

Notes to self:

Life Cycles

Year	Single Digit	Life Events	Age	Single Digit
___	☐		___	☐
___	☐		___	☐
___	☐		___	☐
___	☐		___	☐
___	☐		___	☐
___	☐		___	☐
___	☐		___	☐
___	☐		___	☐
___	☐		___	☐

Your Life Cycle will help you identify the most common single-digit in your pattern that has affected your life experiences. What are your most Life Cycle patterns number # _____? (see the Integrated Master Numerology Expanded Definition at the end of the book).

What is that you learned about yourself?

MASTERY TAKEAWAY

Masterful Creation

ENERGY: 33 is the Energy of creation, the most powerful to achieve.

KNOWLEDGE: The mastery within the 33 empowers you to master your expanded reality.

WISDOM: Use this active energy deliberately, and continue to create your desired reality. Know you are a creator, and you have the free will to create. Focus on what will benefit you most under this amplified energy and trust in your abilities to achieve your preferred experiences.

QUANTUM PHYSICS THUS REVEALS A BASIC ONENESS OF THE UNIVERSE
- ERWIN SCHROEDINGER

SPIRIT PURE

Your Source Connection

Making The Connection

By now I have a profound relationship with the numbers. Numbers are recognized as the universal language.

"Mathematics is the language with which God has written the universe," - Galileo.

Your Source Code

Your Source Code is your multi-dimensional energetic field connection. I've learned how to experience my Source Codes through the numbers. Based on what I've learned along this journey, I realized we have our own unique source coders. Numbers connect us all and transcend language barriers. We do not have communication barriers with numbers. Collectively, we understand the value in numbers the same way.

The Value Of Numbers In Our Lives

To fully understand the importance of your source coder you need to know about the Universal Communicative Codes – UCC. UCC is the energetic string that connects the physical earthly everyday experience to the nonphysical energy. I had to learn the UCC language to fully appreciate the mastery in numbers. The UCC holds the components that affect our etheric and physical experiences.

Tool# 5: Universal Communicative Code, UCC

What Did Tesla Know About 3-6-9?

It's been said that Nikola Tesla would only stay in hotel rooms with room numbers that were divisible by three. Why 3-6-9? Tesla was known for his obsession with 3-6-9. He is quoted as saying:

"If you only knew the
magnificence of the 3, 6 and 9
then you would have the key
to the universe"

-Nikola Tesla

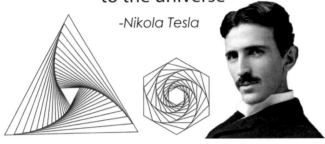

One morning during meditation, out of nowhere Tesla's obsession with 3-6-9 weighed heavily on my mind. I saw the numbers were separated like the image below. I realized I was given more information about the numbers. 3-6-9 are the aspect we affect in the physical; the 1-2-4-5-7-8 are the energetic bond that corresponds to the non-physical.

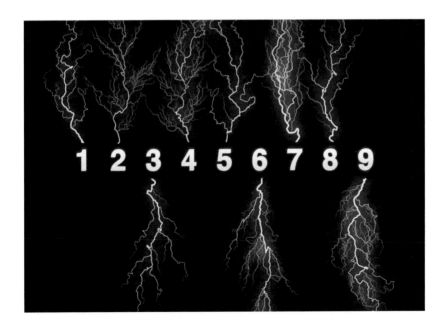

1-2-4-5-7-8 **Etheric Energy** - Mind, Duality, Spirit, Balance, Knowledge, Power

3-6-9 **Physical experience4** – Create, Energy, Source (4 means Spirit)

I think instinctually Tesla knew the energetic meaning of 3-6-9 "Create Energy Source." What if we all walked around with the knowledge that we are creating energy source? Life definitely would be empowering. If you learn how to make it work in a way that serves your ultimate desires, you can live a joyful, connected life. I believe in our ability to create at will. Removing all limitations and human conditions enable you to fully experience free will.

Energetic Field

The Etheric Energy and Physical Energetic Field is a numerically based energy coding system. This system holds you in commune with your greater knowing and your free will. It's like your vibrational armor or your light body. The image helps demonstrate how the energy field is strung through your creations.

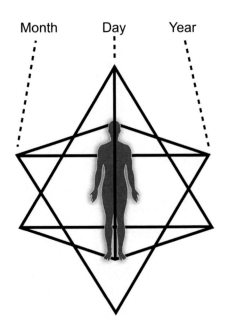

Month   Day   Year

Tool# 6: Polarity

Source Creator "God" gave us all free will. You are free to your will and you have polarity to help your expansion experience. To truly appreciate and understand the magnificent power of your free will, you should seek to understand polarity. This will help you choose the way you experience or observe life.

Polarity governs every decisions. Whatever you are experiencing consciously or unconsciously, polarity affects your overall experience. Your decisions or your interpretations, whether positive or negative, fall on the polarity scale (see examples below). You may choose to look at things in an empowering way, or in a dis-empowering way. It is all your free will! Life can throw some serious curve-balls. Challenges are opportunities to ask yourself: "What's the best way to look at this situation? How can this work for my greatest and highest good?" Those two examples are from an empowering point of view. In the same situation, most are more prone to ask themselves "Why does this always happen to me? Things never work out for me, I always get the worst end of the stick." Same exact experience two different ends of the polarity stick.

In the polarity effect, you have the positively charged mindset or the less empowering, fear-based mindset. Be extremely mindful which end of the stick you choose.

Polarity Stick

What serves you

What does not serve you

+ — **—**

Additive

Subtractive

Positively charged

Negatively charged

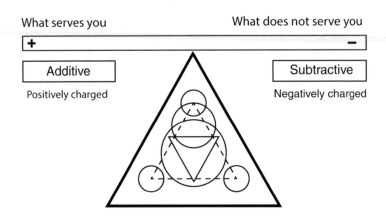

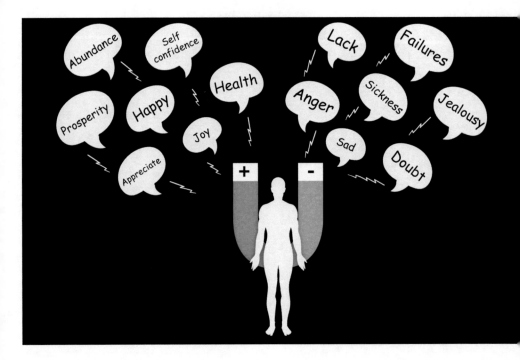

What have you observed?

MASTERY TAKEAWAY

Spiritual Guidance

ENERGY: 44 is the Energy of spiritual connection, the commune with your spirit group.

KNOWLEDGE: The mastery within the 44 is the direct string of communication to your spiritual family.

WISDOM: This beautiful vibr5ation (5 means harmonizing) is strong with intuition and guidance. Trust when you feel a nudge to do something or take action.

THE PHYSICISTS ARE COMING TO THE SAME CONCLUSION THAT THE MYSTICS HAD-THAT IT IS JUST THE VIBRATION FROM WHICH EVERYTHING CAME INTO BEING.

- DR. PILLAI

NEW BEGINNING
AND NATURE
CALLING

Harmonizing The Numbers

Integrated Master Numerology Birth Code Marker has 12 numerical values - 6 Etheric Energy Codes and 6 Perception Ladder Codes. The codes are based on the calculations of your date of birth. These codes reveal a lot about your physical and non-physical Energy, Frequency, and Vibration. Once the numbers are broken down, you can see how the codes are working and affecting your life.

If you share the same birthday with someone, each of you would have different life experiences and interpretations based on your free will. The effect of free will through polarity may allow you to breeze through the impact of a situation, while the other person may experience more challenges. It's all based on how you choose to experience life.

A significant consideration to keep in mind is that we are multi-dimensional beings. Two people may be in the same room, and each will have their own unique experience. We are all vibrational beings; mastering our vibration is the key to achieving mastery within.

Tool #7: IMN Sequencing Chart

Etheric Definitions

The word Ether or Etheric represents an unseen realm. The "Ether" is not just up there or out there but also within. We all have an etheric body. This subtle aspect is referred to as "Linga Sarira" in Sanskrit, and Merkabah in Kabbalah. The etheric body holds the charged connection to the non-physical. It's the energy you were born with, the energy that governs your overall human experience.

To determine your Etheric Energy, use your date of birth in the chart provided. Each number in the chart carries its own individualized characteristics. Etheric Energy has six attributing energies, the significance of each are listed below:

Life Number: Your dominant energy for this lifetime. The attributes of your Life Number influence your personality and governs your path.

Entry Point: Your energetic point of entrance into this lifetime. Your energy doorway into the physical experience.

Event Cycle: The energy that impacts the way event cycles and lesson patterns into your life.

Collective Energy: Your collective connected energy that aligns you to all under the same numeric energy.

Soul Energy: The numeric energy that's imprinted on your soul, Your driving force in this lifetime.

Anchoring Energy: Your combined energy that contributes to the expansion experience. It's the aspect that is associated with your Akash, your legacy energy. (The sum of all the numbers in the Etheric Energy reduced to a single digit, unless if there's a master number.)

Reduce all numbers to a single digit unless a double-digit is present such as 11- 22 -33 - 44, etc.

Example : Tesla's Date of Birth 07-10-1856

ETHERIC ENERGY

| 7 | + | 1 | + | 2 | = | 1 |
| Month | | Day | | Year | | |

ENTRY POINT

| 7 | + | 1 | = | 8 |
| Month | | Day | | |

EVENT CYCLE

| 2 | = | 2 |
| Year | | |

COLLECTIVE VIBRATION

| 7 | + | 2 | = | 9 |
| Month | | Year | | |

SOUL VIBRATION

| 1 | + | 2 | = | 3 |
| Day | | Year | | |

ANCHORING VIBRATION

THE SUM OF ALL THE NUMBERS = 5

Etheric Energy

ETHERIC ENERGY

( ) + ( ) + ( ) = ( )
Month   Day   Year

ENTRY POINT

( ) + ( ) = ( )
Month   Day

EVENT CYCLE

( ) = ( )
Year

COLLECTIVE VIBRATION

( ) + ( ) = ( )
Month   Year

SOUL VIBRATION

( ) + ( ) = ( )
Day   Year

ANCHORING VIBRATION

THE SUM OF ALL THE NUMBERS = ( )

What have you observed?

Perception Ladder

The Perception Ladder is the attribute of the flow of energy into your physical experiences. It exposes the way you experience and interpret your physical expression. This aspect displays the many facets that are influencing you in the way you experience life. It demonstrates your tendencies and the many ways the energy reflects your free will.

To determine your Perception Ladder Energy, use your date of birth in the chart provided. Each number in the chart carries its own individualized characteristics. Perception Ladder energies have six attributing energy, the significance of each are listed below:

Your perception: The way you see life, relate to things and express experiences.

You are perceived: The way others see you and how others relate to you energetically.

Equalizing Vibration: What keeps you balanced, your energy stabilizer.

Effected Vibration: The cause and affect energy, your accountability energy.

Working Vibration: The power energy at work with you. Your charged energy ready to empower your physical experiences.

Mastery Perception Potential: This energy demonstrates the mastery potential flowing to you during this lifetime. This requires a keen sense of self and awareness of your higher potential. The observation of this code reveals your life's potential and purpose. This is your activation key to accessing and achieving your mastery within. (The sum of all the numbers in the Perception Ladder reduced to a single digit, unless if there's a master number.)

Reduce all numbers to a single digit unless a double-digit is present such as 11- 22 -33 - 44, etc.

Example : Tesla's Date of Birth 07-10-1856

YOUR PERCEPTION

[7] + [7]　　　　　= [5]
Month　　Month

YOU ARE PERCEIVED

[1] + [1]　　　　　= [2]
Day　　　Day

EQUALIZING ENERGY

[2]　　　　　　　　= [2]
Year

EFFECTED ENERGY

[7] + [1]　　　　　= [8]
Month　　Day

WORKING ENERGY

[2] + [2] + [2]　= [6]
Year　　Year　　Year

MASTERY PERCEPTION POTENTIAL

(ADD ALL THE NUMBERS ABOVE) = [5]

Perception Ladder

YOUR PERCEPTION

( ) + ( ) = ( )

Month   Month

YOU ARE PERCEIVED

( ) + ( ) = ( )

Day   Day

EQUALIZING ENERGY

( ) = ( )

Year

EFFECTED ENERGY

( ) + ( ) = ( )

Month   Day

WORKING ENERGY

( ) + ( ) + ( ) = ( )

Year   Year   Year

MASTERY PERCEPTION POTENTIAL

(ADD ALL THE NUMBERS ABOVE) = ( )

IMN Brief Definitions

1 You are God "The I Am"

Acknowledge the God in you

**11 God here and on the other side
Acknowledgment of your Source Creator**

To align with your God essence

**2 You and the other side of the veil
"Your higher self"**

Inner guidance

22 Connection of the two and the blend

Being in alignment and accord with your
Higher self

**3 Mother - Father - Child
"Aspect of creation, the Trinity"**

To know that you are creator

**33 The family is together the most powerful
To achieve**

Creating with Divine essence of your
Creator Source

4 Spirit pure

You are not alone Spirit Energy is strong
In your vibration.

44 All spirits are together with loving support

In commune with your spirit group

5 New beginning & nature calling

A call to harmonize with yourself and
Your purpose.

55 New beginning in life, spirit and nature

Ebb and flow harmony

6 Energy

The essence of your frequency

66 Physical and non-physical energy

Align with physical and non-physical energetic
Force

7 Knowledge

The ability to connect with esoteric and
non-esoteric knowledge

**77 Secret knowledge and codes
[Science number]**

The ability to connect and align with secret
Mystery knowledge

8 Divine

God code

**88 Unlimited divine connection, the type that
Creates New World-Power**

Working with the God code knowledge

9 Working with God - Source Creator

Guidance from God

**99 Acknowledgement of God's work
Witness beauty - Love & Light**

Align with joy and the beauty of creation

**IMN Expanded Definitions available at the back of the book **

Notes to self:

Bonus Chart

Etheric Energy

ETHERIC ENERGY

[Month] + [Day] + [Year] = [ ]

ENTRY POINT

[Month] + [Day] = [ ]

EVENT CYCLE

[Year] = [ ]

COLLECTIVE VIBRATION

[Month] + [Year] = [ ]

SOUL VIBRATION

[Day] + [Year] = [ ]

ANCHORING VIBRATION

THE SUM OF ALL THE NUMBERS = [ ]

Bonus Chart

Perception Ladder

YOUR PERCEPTION

( ) + ( ) = ( )

Month   Month

YOU ARE PERCEIVED

( ) + ( ) = ( )

Day   Day

EQUALIZING ENERGY

( ) = ( )

Year

EFFECTED ENERGY

( ) + ( ) = ( )

Month   Day

WORKING ENERGY

( ) + ( ) + ( ) = ( )

Year   Year   Year

MASTERY PERCEPTION POTENTIAL

(ADD ALL THE NUMBERS ABOVE) = ( )

MASTERY TAKEAWAY

Renew To Balance

ENERGY: 55 is an amplified harmonizing energy balance of your nature and new beginnings.

KNOWLEDGE: The mastery within the 55 is the Ebb and Flow of harmonizing energy.

WISDOM: Go with the flow, allow what works for you to flow in, and whatever is not in your best interest to flow out. Be open to changes, new beginnings, and opportunities. This energy is about knowing who you are and honoring your best self. Pay attention to what's in your true nature, with a willingness to change. Try not to hang on to things that are not in your best interest. Use your guidance system to help you reflect your values.

EVERYTHING IS ENERGY AND THAT'S ALL THERE IS TO IT. MATCH THE FREQUENCY OF THE REALITY YOU WANT AND YOU CANNOT HELP BUT GET THAT REALITY. IT CAN BE NO OTHER WAY. THIS IS NOT PHILOSOPHY. THIS IS PHYSICS.
- ALBERT EINSTEIN.

ENERGY

Everything Is Energy, Frequency, And Vibration?

Congratulations, you've made it this far into the realm of Integrated Master Numerology. You may find yourself asking: "What is energy? What is frequency? What is vibration?"

What is Energy?
en·er·gy - enərjē
Noun: the strength and vitality required for sustained physical or mental activity.

Energy is the source required for motion in a created action or experience. For example, when you meet someone, and you think; "I do not like, or I like this person's energy." What you are doing is tapping into the person's energy and interpreting whether they are an effective complement to yours. Our energy is the active vitality that keeps us connected within the created reality.

What is Frequency?
fre·quen·cy - frēkwənsē
Noun: the rate at which something occurs or is repeated based on your interpretation of an experience.

Frequency transmits the strength and movement in which something is experienced. If you keep doing the same thing and getting the same undesired result, then - change the action! Changing the action equates to the shift in frequency; i.e. - if you're listening to a radio station that's playing music and you want to listen to talk radio, you will need to change the channel frequency to talk radio.

What is Vibration?
vi·bra·tion - vī'brāSH(ə)n
Noun: an instance of vibrating.

Vibration is the interpreted emotion; it's how you feel and what you radiate out. Your Vibration shows through your emotional state, the atmosphere of a place, your associations with an object, and felt through your verbal and non verbal actions.

Mind's Eye Perspective:

This is the best example I was shown in a vision about Energy, Frequency, and Vibration.

Imagine a computer. The electrical outlet it's plugged into is it's source of energy. The computer, is the processor, which is the frequency. What you see on the screen is the vibration. The energy is the source that drives or fuels the actions (the outlet or a battery pack). The program you are running is the frequency. What you interpret from the screen is the vibration.

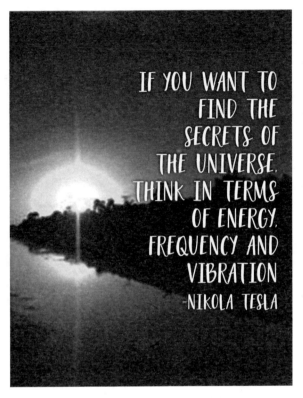

IF YOU WANT TO FIND THE SECRETS OF THE UNIVERSE, THINK IN TERMS OF ENERGY, FREQUENCY AND VIBRATION
-NIKOLA TESLA

Energy charges - frequency transmits-vibration projects: What you do with your understanding of this knowledge is your choice. You may connect to a higher charged energy source or a lower charged energy source in the way you choose to experience life. It's in the way you choose to see things, whether positively or negatively. I've come to appreciate the power in not judging. Decisions people make should not be judged since we don't know their source. Every created reality plays its part. It's all part of the polarity effect and our free will. Every action thought, and emotion are relevant; one could not exist without the other. If someone chooses to connect to a lower source, it may serve them well. However, there's more to be gained if you connect to a higher energy source.

Say this abundance affirmation daily to experience prosperity in your life:

> *I am connected to my abundance Energy*
> *I've raised my wealth Frequency*
> *I am flowing in my prosperity Vibration*

MASTERY TAKEAWAY

Flowing Energy

ENERGY: 66 is Energy amplified in the physical and non-physical energetic source.

KNOWLEDGE: The mastery within the 66 is the charged up energy to your creative expansion. It is the power source that allows you to go non-stop in the creation process.

WISDOM: Nurture your energy and be mindful of where you're placing it. Some people or circumstances will zap your energy or compromise you. Try to engage with energies that will reciprocate what serves you best. Share and cultivate your energy in a way that will empower your life.

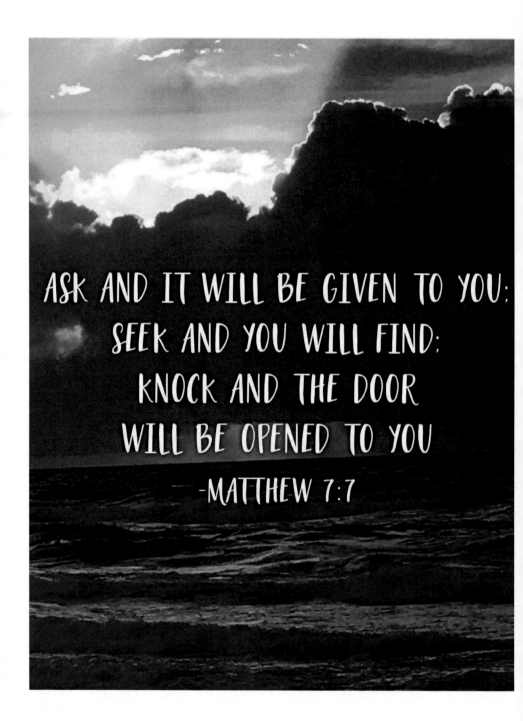

ASK AND IT WILL BE GIVEN TO YOU;
SEEK AND YOU WILL FIND;
KNOCK AND THE DOOR
WILL BE OPENED TO YOU

-MATTHEW 7:7

KNOWLEDGE

The Power Within

During my research for this book, I respected the guidance I was receiving. It occurred to me that all the knowledge I was guided to was always available within me. It was always there to be obtained. I do not feel unique because I made the connection with this unique numeric wisdom. I believe because we the collective are now ready with the capacity to understand this knowledge, I was able to make the connection because we are ready. What affects one, affects all.

The Gospel of Thomas

An exciting and interesting find along my research was the Gospel of Thomas, which again supports Integrated Master Numerology.

Lost Gospel of Thomas from the Nag Hammadi Library: The Gospel of Thomas is mystical and emphasizes a direct and unmediated experience of the truth of life.

Numeric passages interpretation using Integrated Master Numerology:

*Jesus said, **"Where there are three gods, they are gods. Where there are two or one, I am with him."***

The "three gods" are: (3) Trinity (The Mother, Father, Child) the aspect of creation. "Where there are two or one" is the (2) Duality (1) I Am. "I am with him" which suggests being within. This passage is about the nature of our spirit and our connection to the oneness through the I Am, Duality, and Creation.

*Jesus said, **" For there are five trees for you in Paradise which remain undisturbed summer and winter and whose leaves do not fall. Whoever becomes acquainted with them will not experience death."***

The "five trees" represent 5 - New beginning and Nature Calling, which is a passage about change, and the nature of the self. A call to harmonize to achieve enlightenment.

Anytime Jesus begins a statement with the words "I am," we can be sure he is speaking as the Christ, the spiritual beingness that is the truth of who he is, and who we are. We are spiritually one with all creations.

St. Augustine of Hippo (A.D. 354–430), wrote:

"Numbers are the Universal language offered by the deity to humans as confirmation of the truth."

Different Systems In Numerology

Different types of numerology are used all over the world. There are many types of mystical techniques that other cultures attach to numbers. The practices range from:

- The Tibetan Numerology, the oldest form of numerology.
- The Abjab Numeral System, where each alphabet has a numeric value.
- Ki, an ancient Japanese system based upon numerology patterns in the birth date.
- The Hebrew Kabbalah has its own numeric systems.
- In Africa, they use numbers for prediction purposes.
- The Chinese Numerology believes in the double digits even numbers because they believe good things come in two.
- The more predominant is the Chaldean and Pythagorean systems, commonly used in the West, because of ease in practice.

Letters And Their Number Attribute

All letters correspond with a numerological value. The following alphabet and its numerical values are based on the European Numerology used since Roman times. Use the chart to find the letters in your name and their numeric value. See the example that shows exactly how to add up your full name. (I suggest you use the name you most identify yourself with or the name you are most commonly called.)

Tool #8 Letters Numerology

PYTHAGOREAN NUMEROLOGY

A B C D E F G H I
1 2 3 4 5 6 7 8 9

J K L M N O P Q R
1 2 3 4 5 6 7 8 9

S T U V W X Y Z
1 2 3 4 5 6 7 8

J O H N   P E T E R   S M I T H
1 6 8 5   7 5 2 5 9   1 4 9 2 8

$$= \underline{7\,2}$$
$$= \underline{7 + 2}$$
$$= \boxed{9}$$

Knowledge Is Power!

Are you prepared and willing to seek your own knowledge? We are all in search of something; what are you searching for? To note, our modern education system and many other forms of knowledge-based teachings are all relevant. However, we hold the power to guide ourselves toward our own divine sense of knowing. I'm not just referring to the esoteric aspect of understandings. The power resides in knowing what you are searching for is within. My deepest desire is to direct you to the knowledge of self. Applied knowledge of the self is empowerment!

Meditation & Prayer

The beauty in creation lies in the balance. The balance that exists between prayer and meditation can be viewed in their feminine and masculine energy attributes. Prayer is the masculine energy exchange. Meditation is the feminine energy exchange. They complement each other because of their active and receptive nature. In your prayers, you speak (active energy); in your meditation, you listen (receptive energy). Prayers are about you sending out your intentions of gratitude or requests for help. In meditation, you learn to listen and focus your mind to allow energy to respond and flow to and through you. Both practices should be done together to reap their immense benefits.

Self-Guided Meditation

One morning during a guided meditation, I found the meditation annoying. I thought to myself "Why am I doing this? Why can't I just quiet my mind myself?" I took off the earphones, and I quieted my mind.

Tool #9 Energy Center Meditation

During my meditation, I was guided to run the double-digit numbers (11-22-33-44-55-66-77-88- 99) over the center of my body to help me focus and balance. I felt this pull to start at the crown of my head and move down all the way to the soles of my feet. I had a slight ego conflict… I thought that's just the Chakras. The images kept coming until I took notice of the energetic vibration from my knees; which are not part of the Chakra points. I ran the numbers up and down my body and stayed focused on each point. Once I was in alignment, I felt a surge of energy vibrating through my whole body.

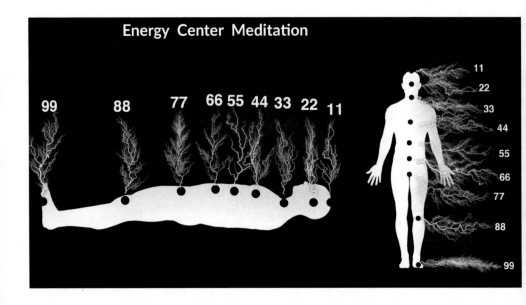

While I was meditating, I was guided to the meaning and energetic value for each point. I was guided to see that I was in an energy center meditation, which helped me identify different points of my body that may be out of alignment or that's holding trapped energy. It's truly powerful!

11	Crown	Light Connection
22	Third Eye	Gateway Access
33	Throat	Expression Field
44	Heart	Emotion Balance
55	Solar	Charge-Off Point
66	Sacral	Power-Point
77	Root	Wisdom
88	Knees	Exchange
99	Sole	Grounding

This is how I worked with the numbers in this self-guided meditation. I started at the top of my head, I breathed into that part of my body attempting to align with the energetic points. I ran the numbers 11 – 99 focusing on each point that I was guided to balance. During the process, I was open to hearing what came while I focused. I took six breaths for each point, I alternated my breath in and out and remained present with my mind, and my breath. I did the same for all the other points. Each time, I felt a block in a point, I'd focus my breath longer until I understood why the resistance. By the time I got to the third full body flow, I was in deep meditation. I got in deeper and faster than I've ever experienced in a guided meditation.

Try this magnetically charged self-guided meditation. Go within, plug in and get connected!

Channeled Message From My Meditation:

You are not an energetic puppet. No energetic beings are controlling you. Guess what? You're the master, you are in control of your experiences. You hold and control the energetic strings. As you project your energy string from within, you connect and align with other energies. You are the master of your experiences; it all starts from within. Your mastery is within. This self-guided meditation will help you tap into your inner being. Blessings

MASTERY TAKEAWAY

The Power In Peace

ENERGY: 77 is the Energy secret knowledge and codes with the ability to connect and align with hidden secret mysteries.

KNOWLEDGE: The mastery within the 77 is a strong connection to cryptic knowledge and understandings.

WISDOM: This higher perspective connection holds the secret to our realities as we see them. It's the knowledge that most do not have the foresight to seek. There's a level of responsibility with working with the 77 energy. May you hold and respect the integrity of the power that's in peace.

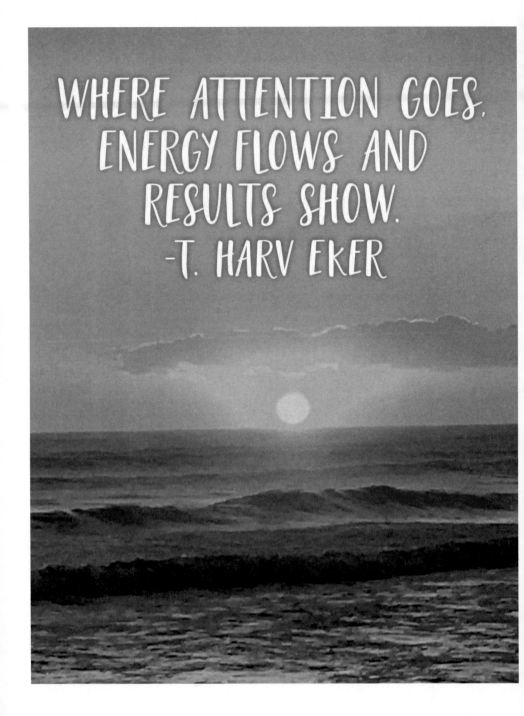

DIVINE

Infinite, God's Code Connection

Daily Co-Created Expressions

Relationship, Money & Home

God's Code is active in our lives. Most of us go through life unaware of the effects the energy of numbers have on us. We tend to make unconscious decisions based on our societal conditioning. We allow un-focused life situations to dictate our experiences. It's a good idea to learn a few tools to help you create consciously. Numerology is one of the tools I use daily to help me process and interpret energies as I experience it. The power in the preciseness in numbers, shows that we are not a crapshoot. We are one with Creator and we are creators; creators of our experiences and realities. We are divine, infinite, God's code for the purpose of expanded expression.

Energetic Tools

The tools available in the collective enable us to create, manage, and quantify our physical experiences. Integrated Master Numerology is one of the tools that has the potential to empower us. IMN helps us to deliberately connect to the quantum field and allows us to experience desired outcomes. We are able to create consciously based on the numeric attributes active in the energy field of the numbers. While there are many other numerology-based practices, none focuses on the awareness of the Quantum factor. The awareness of the amplified double digit of a number assures a certain level of energetic connection and yields desired results in your created reality. The Integrated Master Numerology process connects the physical and non-physical through alignment and makes it one.

How To Make The Two - One?

Integrated Master Numerology system is about understanding the numeric attribute of numbers 1-9 and 11-99. With focused attention, we need to find the alignment to the vibration of the numbers. We can achieve the connection while meditating with the IMN Self-guided meditation or with a focused IMN awareness daily practice. IMN shows how to make the numeric connection to help us understand the many ways the numbers work. The Two becomes One when you remove the separation of the physical and non-physical and apply awareness.

Numbers Daily

We share three common interests - money, love, and health. Most of us spend countless hours and money to get advice and guidance concerning these subjects. Let's examine relationship, money, and home. I've made the conscious decision not to investigate health as I do not feel equipped to approach the subject.

Relationships

It's important to keep a balanced relationship with our loved ones, friends, co-workers, etc. A cohesive, balanced relationship will bring you happiness, and peace of mind. Most are not aware of the numeric impacts in relationships. The Energy, Frequency, and Vibration of a relationship cycle are a relevant component of the expanded experience.

The numeric cycle in a relationship in Integrated Master Numerology works like this; let's explore the different cycles. You've just met someone; the first year is associated with the newness of that relationship...

Year 1: can be viewed like a child's developmental experience; you are learning new things about the person. You are getting to know different characteristics as you both navigate this new experience. While exploring the "I am-ness" within this new connection you have the opportunity to examine yourself within this new relationship.

Year 2: is the duality is how you are experiencing the different sides. Is it fitting your desired outcome and expectations? An examination that's always present even when you are not aware of the duality in nature.

Tool # 10 Relationship Cycles And Attributes 1-9

1. Newness individualized
2. The sides you are reflecting to each other
3. What we are creating together
4. Connection intention
5. Does this relationship work? Will it work?
6. The aspect keeping us together
7. What you know about the other person
8. The factors that are keeping the relationship active
9. The trust process (does the relationship stay active or dissolve?)

The time to look at the relationship cycle is when an emotion appears; you need to examine the source of the energetic fueled vibration. All relationships have a cycle, and the cycles may be interpreted through the IMN definitions. Use the IMN definition chart to help identify the cycle attributes. When a relationship is in the double-digit number such as 15 (1+5=6) or 13 (1+3=4). That's how you reduce double-digits to a single digit. Do not reduce to single digit if a double-digits like 11 -22- 33 etc. are present. Refer to Age Chart to better aid with number reduction.

The numeric values applies to all phases of a relationship. The energy holds the value of the number whether you're in a one day or a one-year connection; three days or three-year relationship. Follow the IMN numeric attribute to understand the vibration within your co-created relationships.

Money

Money Is Energy!

Money is the most commonly used form of energy exchange. We agree and understand that money is important. While money is a taboo subject for some and a dedicated focus for others, no matter how we view money, we all need it. The power we've placed on money has enabled it to be its own influential energy. Vibrant energy at that! This energy impacts each and everyones' experiences. Money is even used to manipulate us into compliance and conformity.

The concentration and motivation we place on money are powerful. It's a good idea to be mindful of your personal feelings about money. The way you choose to experience money effects the Energy, Frequency, and Vibration of the way it flows in your life. Money may be viewed as a friend or a foe. I know someone who would always say to his kids "We don't talk about money, that's rude!" Now, what's the message being imprinted in those young minds? The other common statement is "Money is the root of all evil." So many of us grew up having limiting beliefs impressed in our psyche. How wrong are those limiting beliefs?

Let's go on a journey to identify the Energy, Frequency and Vibration concerning money. The following exercises require a keen focus on some of your imprinted views. Take a moment for this self-examination. At the end of the process, you'll be able to identify the effect at work concerning your relationship with the money. This process will help point out some of your views, which will help you identify ways to make money work for your desired outcome.

Tool #11 Money Relationship

Money Energy

Think as far back as you can. What are your money beliefs? Where did they originate? Use the chart below to write down your answers, narrowing your beliefs to the most dominant.

See examples to help demonstrate the process:

Money Beliefs

1 Money doesn't grow on trees

1 I need to work hard for money

2 I need to work hard for money

1 I need to work hard for money

2 Money doesn't make you happy

3 Money doesn't make you happy

Money Beliefs

1 _____

                   1 _____

2 _____

                                                1 _____

                   2 _____

3 _____

Read over your list. Where do your money beliefs stem from? Are those beliefs serving you?

What have you learned about your money energy ?

Notes to self:

Money Frequency

Money Cycle

You've identified your money beliefs. Now let's examine how money shows up in your life. Think of at least 3 or 9 maximum memorable money events (The events do not have to be in order). Money Cycle is your relationship patterns concerning money. This process will show you how money shows up in your experience and the numeric attributes associated with your beliefs. Write down your memorable money events, it will help you see the frequency you've attached to yourself concerning money.

See example to help demonstrate the process:

Example

Money Cycles

Year	Single Digit	Life Events	Age	Single Digit
2000	2	Got married to money	30	3
1988	8	Got money from my parents for college	18	9
1995	6	Got a friend from college to help pay my bills while I finished school	25	7
1997	8	Got a good paying job	27	9
2005	3	Me and my husband took an extended vacation to Europe	35	8
1987	7	Got college scholarship	17	8
2010	3	Got Divorced	40	4
2013	6	Went back to work	43	7
2015	8	Got inheritance	45	9

In this example, you can see that 8 numeric energy dominates her money cycle, 3, and 7 are her secondary influences. Write down your money cycle and look for your numeric energy influences.

Money Cycles

Year	Single Digit	Life Events	Age	Single Digit
_____	☐		_____	☐
_____	☐		_____	☐
_____	☐		_____	☐
_____	☐		_____	☐
_____	☐		_____	☐
_____	☐		_____	☐
_____	☐		_____	☐
_____	☐		_____	☐
_____	☐		_____	☐

Read over your list. What do you think about your money frequency? Check within for the feelings you have associated with what you've written.

What have you learned about your money frequency?

Money Vibration

The money vibration is associated with how you feel and your emotions attached to the way you experience money. The previous money relationship processes helped you identify some fundamental money beliefs and experiences. With the knowledge gained from the previous exercises, you can examine the role you played in the way you manifested money. To identify your vibration, use the Money Cycle to examine your associations. The chart below will help you narrow down your associations to the most dominant.

See examples to help demonstrate the process:

Example

Money Associations

1 I need money to pay my bills

2 extra — I need money to do anything

1 I need money to pay my bills

1 I need money to pay my bills

2 Respect & security

3 Respect & security

Money Associations

1 _____

2 _____

3 _____

1 _____

2 _____

1 _____

Read over your list. Do you think what you're projecting energetically about money serves you? Examine the feelings that are associated with what you've written.

What have you learned about your money Vibration?

Money Energy Management

The process you've just completed gives you the opportunity to see your relationship with money. The deliberate observation is the key to achieving the desired results. The best quantum statement I've ever heard came from the show *Futurama*. In the episode there was a horse race, the announcer: "It's a dead heat, they are checking the Electron microscope – and the winner is number 3 in a quantum finish. They're checking the Electron microscope." One of the characters betting on the race responded with, "No fair, you changed the outcome by measuring it!!" When I saw that clip I couldn't help but laugh. Such a poignant response to the effect of accurate observation. I loved it! The statement was "no fair, you changed the outcome by measuring it!!" That is precisely what I aim to do when it comes to the IMN process. Measuring the numbers will enable us to affect the observed experience outcome in a way that serves us best.

Notes to self:

Home

My exposure to numerology also started my fascination into house numbers. I would drive through neighborhoods and wonder, what's the house number saying about what's going on in the home? When the home looks in disarray from the outside or when the home is too immaculate, I wondered what life was like inside the home. I did that for years, I never really remembered to look for the definitions of the houses.

Now I have a better understanding of what's at work in association with a house number. For this example, I will use a house that has the 3 Energy. The way to calculate the house number is to add up the address to a single digit such as 12 (1+2=3). The 3 is the aspect of creating. Let's say you live in a house with that number, you have a unique opportunity to create wonderful things and experiences. Remember, polarity is always at work. The same way there's the potential to create beauty, the opposite possibilities also are available. If in this home you feel underprivileged, the more lack you will create. Once you are aware of your home numeric attributes and potential effects, you can make conscious decisions on how to observe and experience your house energy. See image for how to reduce house number

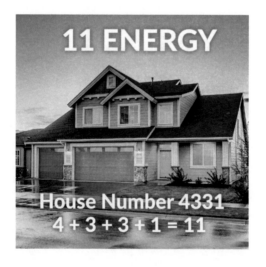

Tool #12 Home Energy

The *mother lode* number for a home is 11. This house number, like all the other master numbers, does not get reduced. An 11 house is a fully charged enlightened lighthouse. Your enlightenment may be positively or negatively charged. The beauty in this house number is the extra charged energy. It brings awareness to your life within this home.

When I moved into a home that was a 5-energy , I was aware it represented a new beginning and call to nature (my nature and the nature of everyone in the home). I made sure nothing stayed stagnate. I moved around my furniture all the time. I decluttered my home often. I was mindful of who I let inside and monitored the condition in which they came. I was determined not to create new situations I was not willing to see through or experience.

Life In The Home

We all experience life based on our point of reference and observations. Two people from the same home could have two separate and distinct experiences in the same household. This is based on the Energy, Frequency, and Vibration they've attuned to in the house. Ever talk to siblings that were raised in the same home? They may each have different accounts of their experiences. A family that's in agreement remains in cooperation with shared memories. A disconnected family will have different memories and experiences.

MASTERY TAKEAWAY

Manifesting

ENERGY: 88 is the Energy unlimited universal divine connection, the type that creates new world.

KNOWLEDGE: The mastery within the 88 is power! It works with God's code of expansion. This infinite energy is the continuous movement and evolution of creation.

WISDOM: Working with God's Code is an expansion experience. Within this energy, there are the potentials to effect and activate your preferred reality. This energy is life's constant evolution and regeneration. Be open to your immense abundance possibilities.

THE KEY TO GROWTH IS THE INTRODUCTION OF HIGHER DIMENSIONS OF CONSCIOUSNESS INTO OUR AWARENESS.
- LAO TZU

WORKING WITH GOD – SOURCE CREATOR

Integrated Master Numerology

Why Integrated Master Numerology?

Integrate means to combine one thing with another so they can become whole. The Integrated part of this process is to be one with the Energy, Frequency and Vibrational attributes of the numbers that are active in your life. Master Numerology observes the double-digit aspect of numerology, which carries unique characteristics and amplified powers. You put them together, and you get the unified connection to your Source Creator. Working with God (a.k.a.

Prime Creator or Source Creator) is about your alignment to Joy, Happiness and Blessings. Trust God and allow good things to flow into your life.

Quantum Connection

I'm about to get a bit Nerdy... please stay with me. Let's use the double slit experiment, probably the most recognized experiment in physics that demonstrates unmatched strangeness. Imagine, tiny particles of matter with some degrees of waves. Observing them has a noticeable effect on their behavior. The very act of observing is incredible. Measuring them causes the particle to surrender the probability of all the places it could go and forces it to pick one location. This is precisely what the IMN practice aims to help you achieve. This tool once mastered gives you the potential to affect probabilities in your favor.

The Law Of Attraction

Law of Attraction govern us with rigid accountability to our vibration because what we put out we get back. The aspect of like attracts like is definite. We tend to say opposites attract, but that could not be further from the truth. I gained that understanding in a Kabbalah book about relationships by Dr. Yehuda Berg, The Spiritual Rules of Engagement. This book opened my eyes to the masculine and feminine attraction and alignment. For the feminine energy to achieve alignment to the masculine energy, that energy had to allow the flow of the unified connection. My biggest takeaway was the concept of like attracts like, and opposites repel. I love the way the book describes God's perfection and the relationship between the energies seeking to find alignment.

My Truth!

It all started with me asking for truth. I wanted an external truth, along the way I discovered my own inner truth. I no longer needed the truth that embodied someone else's experience. My deliberate observations using the numbers enabled me to align with what was in my best interest and to my point of connection to my Source. At the end of it all, my most prized truth is empowerment. My empowerment allows me to be at peace with myself and to respect others for their choices. I appreciate and understand we are all loving extensions of Source having our unique human experiences.

Notes to self:

MASTERY TAKEAWAY

God's Love

ENERGY: 99 is the Energy that acknowledges God's work

KNOWLEDGE: The mastery within the 99 is to appreciate and witness the Beauty, Love and Light of God's creation. Trust in the process and know your Source is Love.

WISDOM: We are all an extension of the Prime Creator – God. The beauty in creation is that we are part of the created experience. We're not here to wait for something to happen to us; We are here to make things happen. May you read this statement over, and over again until you can understand this message. Witness beauty – Love and Light.

Mind's eye
My narrated conversation with God

The stillness of Source Creator-God was silent, calm, peaceful and loving. An existence that was complete and whole. In the beginning, there was the I Am of existence. Then, came Duality in the experience. They played alongside each other with love, pure bliss, and joy. One day as if in a game of hide and seek, he moved to the other side of the vail. She looked everywhere for her dual self. He was nowhere in the physical. She was so lonely, sad, and unable to see him in spirit. His non-physical experience was working on the other side to help her create new experiences with his loving and guiding support. Her sadness was too deep for her to see the beauty that was created for her to experience. Her grief was so profound in her perceived loss, she sunk into low consciousness. Her head hung low on a rock, and she created low energy thoughts like fear of being alone, lost, betrayal, and emptiness. From the other side, he created high energy like dolphins, whales, flowers, the rivers that led to the sea, the sun that shined on her, and the land animals that came to play with her to keep her company. Her pain was too deep and she couldn't acknowledge the beauty around her. Gifts after gifts, her head remained low on the rock. Many low energies kept coming out of her sorrows. Millions of years went by with her head hung low.

One day, a butterfly got her attention then she realized she may not be alone. She watched this butterfly with love. Her love was back! She now sees the beauty that surrounds her. She fell in love with life, and she began to live and play with all that was created for her with Love. After years, which turned into centuries and millions of years, she started to question her existence and environment. In the moment of stillness, while observing nature, she connected with her dual self. The awareness of him opened a new door to her physical and nonphysical self.

"In the stillness you find God, in the chaos you find you."
-Daphney Antonie

Conversation with God during my meditation

God:
What are you doing here?

while I was shaking to my core

Me:
I am here to create!

God replies with love:

I place no judgment
upon you, nor should you.

IMN Expanded Definitions

1 Energy is the acknowledgment of The God in you, the "I AM." It calls for you to know your magnificence. The 1 Energy brings new things and experiences. This engages your evolutionary powers and connection with the oneness, God.

1 Leading Energy inspires you to lead, no need to wait for the pack to approve your actions. Lead on, and the rest will follow. Your inabilities to connect with a large group is okay. You're bringing forth newness, the collective energy may not be in alignment with you. The 1 Energy demands your confidence. Seeking validation under this number only limits your full potential. Pay attention to what you are placing after your "I am…" Connect with your oneness. As you observe life, remember your power and connection is within.

1 Energy encourages you to acknowledge the God in you and in everyone. Focus on your abilities to connect with the beauty of the oneness, God. This energy brings empowerment and stewardship to you. This requires confidence and ease of mind to deliver the forward moving new energy experience. Allow the God in you to fully experience your expansions.

"May you see yourself as a leader in the cause, not alone in the experience."

11 Energy is God here and on the other side, the acknowledgment of Source Creator, God. This illuminating energy directs you to align with your Creator. This Energy is your evolutionary power and relationship with the oneness, God. It shows you are ready to see the God inside you.

11 Pillar Energy offers insight into an amplified connection. This leading energy is a reflection of your spiritual enlightenment. The 11 Energy nudges you to seek and find your new level of awareness. As you observe life, remember the power within is your connection with Source Creator.

11 Energy is the reflective Source energy. This energy is like a lighthouse; it brings light wherever it is present.

"May you see yourself as the illuminator within the experience. Where there is light, darkness may not exist!"

2 Energy is your inner guidance, the connection to your higher self. This Energy deals with duality, the relationship with your non-physical. This links to your higher-self as you go through life.

2 Duality Energy prompts you to trust that there is something more significant at work for your benefit. An introspective mindset is vital. Do not rush to decisions, rely on your inner knowing as you navigate through your life. The higher-self connection is not widely known, many are not aware there's a mission control to help you navigate your life. Instead, we struggle to steer our personal experiences. The 2 Energy is the relationship between your physical and non-physical self. This knowledge is vital, because your soul desires access to your non-physical self.

2 Energy doesn't take things at face value. There's a need to see the two sides. This energy encourages you to pursue different facts. The more you explore, the more things will appear. This energy is about dualistic perception and guidance.

"May you run to self and not away from self "

22 Energy is the connection of the two and the blend. This deliberate connection to the higher-self offers the ability, foresight, and knowledge to impact perceptions. This energy is very influential. Your conscious decision to orient yourself and blend with this energy gifts you with immense significance.

22 Melding Energy prompts you to seek the connection to your higher self. This dualistic nature taps into the ability to influence others. The 22 Energy is the alignment and commune with a higher perspective.

22 Energy encourages you to dig deeper. The more you explore within, the more insight you get into the dualistic aspects. This energy amplifies dualistic expression, perception, and guidance.

"May you seek your higher knowing and be receptive to your greater perspectives."

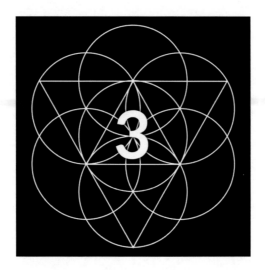

3 Energy is the energy of creation, the Trinity "Mother, Father, Child," the catalyst. This Energy is powerful with the opportunity to continuously create experiences in your life. This "Abracadabra" energy, which you create at will, requires a keen focus on your thoughts and actions.

3 Creation Energy allows you to choose the way you experience life; after all, you have free will! Be aware of your thoughts, the company you keep, your actions, and words. What you associate with in your life has impact. If you choose to feel sorry for yourself, more negativity will come your way. Empowering your thoughts will bring empowering experiences. The 3 Energy supports the way you choose to acknowledge life, which determines the type of reality you create. Know you are a creator, take control of what's in your best interest, and well-being.

3 Energy excites an unwavering desire to create. This energy requires deliberate intention towards what you're generating in your life. You hold the responsibility of your expansion through creation. This shows you are the creator of your reality.

"May you know you have control over your creations. Create
beautiful fun-filled exciting experiences"

33 Energy is the Trinity of the family together and is the most powerful to achieve. This energy empowers you to master your reality. This catalyst is the most powerful to use to create your reality.

33 Powerful Energy is the energy of masterful creation. This helps you create your desires three times stronger than the average life experiences. The 33 Energy supports the Trinity in creation and forms your reality.

33 Energy is the catalyst for expansion through creations. Creating with your divine essence supports the expansion experience.

"May you continue to create at will with full awareness of your power as a creator"

4 Energy is your connection to Spirit Pure. It calls for you to acknowledge the purity in your spiritual connection. This beautiful energy is a pure relationship with your spirit guides.

4 Supporting Energy of Spirit Pure is an active, supportive energy. Seek guidance, and you shall be guided. If you decide to live a disconnected life from spirit, you will experience an uncomfortable feeling of imbalance. Not connecting with that loving guidance will leave you with a sense of void. The 4 Energy is your spiritual support system and loving guidance. Take the time to acknowledge that you are a beautiful spiritual being. Trust when you feel you are being guided by a greater force.

4 Energy is the innate knowledge that will enable you to know you are a Pure Spirit.

"May you allow divine guidance and not try to steer away from the love flowing to you."

44 Energy is all spirits together with loving support. You are in commune with your spirit group. This is the direct communication with your spirit group and is a powerful guidance system.

44 Reinforcing Energy is your compass as you navigate life. This energy is your direct line of heightened connection to Spirit. The 44 Energy is strong with intuition and guidance. Trust when you feel a push to do something or take action.

44 Energy is the enlightened self that supports knowledge for what is best for you. Your inner being always knows what's best; use this elevated connection to enriched your life.

"May you vibrate with the unconditional connection with your spirit guides."

5 Energy is new beginnings and the call to nature. This energy is about harmonizing and discernment. Self-Reflective energy encourages you to be open to change. Pay attention to what's in your true nature. The new beginning is the willingness to let go of what no longer serves you and be open to new experiences. The call to nature is the realization of your personal nature, the real you.

5 Harmonizing Energy is calling you to understand yourself and your purpose. The 5 Energy is a challenging Energy as it requires you to really look at yourself and examine your values. This energy encourages you to drop what no longer is working in your life. It will not serve you to fear letting go; be open to new preferred experiences.

The 5 Energy is about the shift in your experience. It is necessary to consciously change to what's in your best interest. To do so, you must know yourself well.

"May you flow with what works best for you and not with what no longer serves you."

55 Energy is the new beginning in life, spirit, and nature. This is ebb and flow energy. Have keen insights into who you are and your purpose. Harmonizing with yourself, your relationship, and circumstances will yield immense benefits. Honor your spiritual self and pay attention to what's in your true nature.

55 Ebb and Flow Energy is a calling to go with the flow of what's best for you, be open to changes, and new beginnings. Try not to hang on to things that are not in your best interest. This energy is your guidance system to use to reflect your values. The 55 Energy requires you to know yourself and your dispositions.

The 55 Energy is the balance and scale for your life. Creation itself is about the shifting energy; it is necessary to consciously change and adjust to what serves you.

"May you flow out stagnated energy and flow in your vibrant, and active creative energy."

6 Energy is a charged up experience. With its full vigor for life, this spiritedness energy inspires a "Ready Set Go" attitude towards life.

6 Charged Up Energy is an empowering, and energized experience. It encourages the "Can Do It" feeling, and attitude. Underutilizing this energy causes lack of motivation and possible debilitating depression. The 6 Energy is the influence needed to keep things active.

The 6 Energy is power personified and full of life. Everything is energy! Connecting with your energy stream will impact your life.

"May you embrace your energy and keep it active in your life."

66 Energy is the physical and non-physical energy that aligns with your Source, which is essential for your creation experience with God.

66 Aligning Energy is the power to focus on your connections. This energy has the power to positively charge and alter your experiences. The 66 Energy amplifies whatever you're giving attention to in life. Nurture your energy and be mindful of where you're placing your focused attention.

The 66 Energy is an amplified force. Everything is energy! A focused alignment helps cultivate your energy in a way that will empower your life.

"May you experience the energetic power that's in alignment with Source Creator - God."

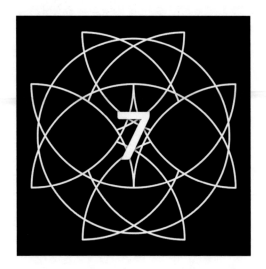

7 Energy is knowledge. This exceptional energy holds the key to interpret the esoteric with greater understanding.

7 Accelerated Knowledge Energy calls for a higher level of mastery. This is the energy of the seeker of truth and the unknown. It offers a broader logical sense with a superior perspective on any subject. The 7 Energy is the connection that enables you to grasp realities that most couldn't recognize.

The 7 Energy is the ability to comprehend life's higher knowledge.

"May you continuously seek awareness that will empower you and not shy away from your inborn gift for knowledge."

77 Energy secret knowledge and codes [Science number]. It connects and aligns with secret mystery knowledge and cryptic information. This higher knowledge offers a deep level of understanding that most wouldn't have the foresight to seek. This mystery connection holds the secret to our realities.

77 Mystery Intelligent Energy connects you to superior perspectives. This is the broader logical sense of the mystery knowledge. The appropriate use of this energy has the potential to make positive contributions to society. The 77 Energy is the energy that can reveal the secret of creation. Deliberate connection to this energy can yield powerful knowledge with the potential to comprehend realities that most people wouldn't or couldn't distinguish.

The 77 Energy is cryptic connection. Based on how this energy is used or the attention it's given, the 77 Energy has the potential to impact or manipulate the reality of the masses.

"May you reach for the higher understanding that will progress and empower your reality."

8 Energy is the Divine God code. This infinite energetic movement is what keeps your experience in a continuous movement. This is life's constant evolution and regeneration.

8 Infinity Energy is the connection to the continued experience. This energy requires a keen focus on what you are keeping active in your life. Try to retain what's in your best interest. The 8 Energy is a continuous movement which helps you expand within the infinite "God's Code."

The 8 Energy is the unified essence essential to the regeneration of life.

"May you expand within your continuous movement and not wander off your path."

88 Energy is a universal Divine connection that creates New World Power! This energy works with God's code and holds the key to its powers. This infinite regenerating energy is a continuous movement and evolution.

88 God's Code Energy is the infinite connection to your reality. This abundance energy requires a focus on what you are keeping active in your life. Holding stagnate energy in your life may block the flow of your potential. The 88 Energy is the moving power within the infinite God's Code of creation.

The 88 Energy is the ability to align with your God's code within. Your understanding of the value of this energy will expand your reality.

"May you connect with your infinite God's Code to help you develop your experience"

9 Energy working with God is the energy that offers guidance. This is also a point of completion, the end of a cycle. At the end of it all, there is always God.

9 God's Connection Energy calls for you to trust that God is working through you, with you, and for you. Not having that trust will create feelings of disconnection and disbelief in the power of creation. The 9 Energy is also the depositing point for your created experience; it holds the key to a completed lesson. The strength of this energy lies in the message that says " Know I Am God."

The 9 Energy is the cohesive and unrelenting connection between you and Source Creator.

"May you trust God and let go."

99 Energy is the acknowledgment of God's work, witness Beauty, Love & Light. This energy welcomes you to align with the joy and beauty of creation. Trust in the process and know your Source is Love.

99 Love Energy Connection calls for you to trust that God's love is working through you, with you, and for you. As you navigate your life, there are energetic drop-off points and a resting spot like in your moment of gratitude. We are part of the beauty in creation. We're not here to wait for something to happen to us; We are here to make things happen. The 99 Energy is the leading off point in a completed process. As cycles end, there are always new ones. Connection to Source under this energy will empower you with love.

The 99 Energy is a loving and empowering connection between you and God. Trust in the process and the beauty of creation. Know this is all God's work!

"May you seek joy and bliss in your created reality."

ACKNOWLEDGMENTS

I conducted an energy experiment with my son, Pearce. We took two of the same things, one we gave love (energy) and the other we ignored (no energy). What happened was astonishing! The one that got love flourished and the other perished. This experiment confirmed to me the value of energy. Which is why I value the people in my life that are always ready to share their loving heart energy with my children and me.

My most valuable energy exchange is with my family. I would not be who I am today without the loving support of my mother, Romaine Esperance, and my sister, Adelaine Antoine. My children, James, I admire your intelligence and look forward to witnessing the many contributions you will make to society. Pearce, you kept me accountable each time you asked me when I was going to be done with the book because you couldn't wait to read it. I love your curious mind and your loving heart, your enthusiasm kept me on track. Chloe, you demonstrate so much strength at such a young age. I'm tremendously proud each time I hear the three of you loving souls call me mom. Stephen, thank you for the many lessons learned through you and for bringing Charlotte and Lauren into my life.

Eileen Augustyn, you inspire me. We met every week during the three years it took for me to write this book. No matter what was going on, you always showed up with the most beautiful zest for life energy. You're truly a powerful woman.

Antony David, my design editor, thank you for your patience and endurance. So many times, I'd get an idea that I hadn't fully formulated. I would message you with the idea, and you would always deliver a design beyond what I had imagined. I am so grateful that you get me and my design ideas. Dawn Southgate, thank you for sharing your sensible perspectives and suggestions. Dr. Zdeslav Hrepic and Sandy Means, thank you for reading the book before I went into the final editing process. Your recommendations and opinions helped shape the energetic flow of the book. Charlyne Schaub, my editor, who knew when I was guided to go to the mystery book store it was to meet you. You are the answer to my prayers. Because the concepts in this book are so complex, I envisioned sitting with someone discussing what I was trying to convey while we edited. That's precisely what we did during our editing sessions. I cannot thank you enough for welcoming me into your home with open heart. We shared many good conversations and laughter while watching Coco (the most exotic cat I've ever seen) get into some fun mischiefs.

My Power Heart Girls, I love you all and thank you. To the wonderful people that supported me and gave me energy while I was working on this book, thank you will never be enough. My heart is filled with joy at the completion of this life-altering project.

Feeling blessed,
Daphney

About Author

Daphney is a loving mother of three beautiful, kind, intelligent and happy children. She holds a degree in International Business. While working on her masters, Daphney was a freelance hair and makeup artist in Miami. During that period, she worked on international fashion campaigns. She fell in love with the glamorous world of fashion, which led to continuing down the path of the fashion and productions, an industry that she excelled in internationally. Working as an international hair and makeup artist for more than 20 years gave her an appreciation for the beauty and fashion industry.

After the birth of her second son, Daphney decided to stop traveling and remain close to her children. During that time, she reconnected to her spiritual life through meditation, a life-altering reconnection.

Daphney is trained in Theta Healing and is a dedicated practitioner of meditation and guided meditation. She keeps a notebook and pen near her bed in case a message gets impressed on her psyche during her moment of stillness. Her goal is to help others find their mastery within.

"The best way to experience God's true beauty in creation is to acknowledge the beauty that is you!" Daphney Antoine

DAPHNEY ANTOINE

www.imnmastery.com